The
POLICE
Application Form
Guide

ISBN: 978-1-291-46589-1
First Published: 2013

Introduction

The Police Application Form Guide was written to help the thousands of budding Police officers out there.

Becoming a Police Officer can be an extremely overwhelming process, after all, a candidate has many aspects of their personality tested rigorously at various stages. One of the most difficult challenges during the lengthy process of becoming a Police Officer is the application form.

Even the most capable and experienced candidates can fall down at the application stage. It is a sad fact of modern recruitment that the best candidates don't always get the job, getting through to interview stage now relies as heavily upon application form technique as it does experience.

This is one of the main reasons that The Police Application Form Guide was written. We want to ensure that the very best candidates do get the job, that those who can demonstrate the necessary attributes required to become a Police officer can showcase their abilities in such a way that will get them noticed by recruitment staff and through to the interview stage, whether they've worked as a Police Special Constable for three years or are a member of the public who possess the necessary qualities.

The guide aims to ensure that nothing about the form is left to chance. It provides the reader with a scientific approach to filling in the form, the security of knowing that they've completed it in such a way that will showcase their experience in the best possible light and will provide them with the best possible chance of progressing through to the interview stage.

Finally, good luck. The road to becoming a Police Officer is often a demanding one. Stay focused. Stay motivated.

Chapter 1

The Application Form – a little background.

"The secret of getting ahead is getting started. The secret of getting started is breaking your complex overwhelming tasks into small manageable tasks, and then starting on the first one."
– Mark Twain

Firstly, congratulations on getting an application form. Getting an application form in the current Police hiring climate is in its self the first hurdle to overcome on the road to becoming a Police Officer.

Candidates like yourself have faced years of recruitment freezes due to tight budgets and Police cut-backs and as such the demand for Police application forms has soared. Added to this Police forces have recently opted to hire in extremely short bursts and often limit application forms to internal candidates only, such as Police Community Support Officers (PCSOs) and Special Constables, rarely opening their doors to the general public.

Not only has this recruitment strategy ensured that it is difficult to get an application form but that the calibre of candidates that you are competing against is high and include highly experienced PCSOs and Special Constables.

Don't let this put you off though! This book will teach you how to level the playing field if you lack direct policing experience or if you have the experience, it will demonstrate how you should frame and structure your answers to achieve the maximum application form score.

So however you've managed to get an application form, whether you're a Police Special Constable, a PCSO or a member of the public, it is extremely important to make your application form as effective as possible to give you the best possible chance of reaching the next stage of the recruitment process.

Chapter 2

Understanding how the form is marked

Knowledge is power.
-Francis Bacon

The police application form is unlike any other form that you will likely have to fill in but by knowing the marking and scoring technique utilised by Police recruiters, as well as following our answer structuring guidelines, it could potentially be the easiest.

Understanding how the form is scored and exactly what the Police recruiters are looking for would give you the ultimate advantage when filling in your form. We provide you with this knowledge, however it is important that you get in to the mind-set of a recruiter when you are fashioning your answers.

Remember, being a Police recruiter is no easy job. You're faced with hundreds of application forms, a looming deadline and large volumes of information that you have to sift through in the quickest possible time and in the most efficient way. So what is your approach? - You compare each and every application form to a standard list of key phrases, you tirelessly read hundreds of answers and try to figure out if they demonstrate the phrases you're looking for, if you see them, you give them a point.

So if this is the recruiters technique and your form is the hundredth form of the day, how should you write to make it easy for them and score highly? Simple, you **take the key phrases directly from their list** and put them in to your form. You take your life experiences relating to the competency question and you tailor it to include the key phrases.

And the best part?

You have these key phrases! They are provided with your application form, I'm referring to the Police Core Competency sheets (they're even in the back of this book). In the following chapters we show you exactly how to **seamlessly integrate the key phrases** in to your personal experiences using our example answers and answer structuring guide.

You must make it your aim in every answer you provide to **make**

it easy for the recruiters looking at your form to pick out the key phrases and skills that they are looking for. Remember at all times to **write for your target audience** – the recruiter**.**

Remember, there is a **formula** for completing these application forms, it's a science. Recruiters are desperately looking for key phrases, so give all of them to them and we'll teach you how.

Getting Technical

Below is how the application form is marked from a technical point of view, you may find it helpful to know these facts but the most important factor to understanding how the form is marked is mentioned on the previous page.

- Applications are given an A to D grade.

- Applications are graded relative to other candidates scores.

- To get an A grade you need to be in the top 15% of candidates.

- To get a D grade you would be in the bottom 15% of candidates.

- There are two ways to progress to interview stage
  1. Get a B grade in 3 out of the 4 sections
  2. Get a B grade in 2 out of the 4 sections and achieve a B grade in you form overall.

- 10 spelling mistakes lead to automatic failure.

Keys to success

- Make it easy for recruiters to pick out key phrases.

- Lift the key phrases directly from the Core Competency booklet.

- Integrate the key phrases seamlessly in to your experiences.

- Follow our winning formula detailed in this book.

Chapter 3

Personal Information

*All parts of society need to feel that the police service is their
police service, and that does not happen unless all parts of
society are represented in the police.*
- Chris Patten

There is little to be gained by teaching you how to fill in the personal information section of the application form as it is just that, personal information.

We recommend that you **hand write** this section, typeface has to be size 12 font which can often leave you struggling to fit in all your details.

In the next chapter we will dive straight in to structuring and writing your competency questions but below are a few tips to ensure that you don't fall down on this relatively simple but time consuming stage.

Keys to success

- Handwrite this section of your application.

- **ALWAYS** write in black ink using a ball point pen.

- Print out at least 3 copies of this section – you will make mistakes.

- Read and re-read your final draft, do not make errors at this stage.

- If you have tattoos, criminal convictions or financial issues that need to be declared, ensure you enclose all relevant documents.

- If you're unsure of anything – call your force's HR.

- Put 'N/A' in any blank areas that do not apply to you.

- When filling in family details, ensure you cross out family member titles that do not apply to you e.g. – 'step-mother' or 'step-sister' etc.

- Take time to read every part of every question carefully and do not rush, it is easy to miss important parts of this section.

Chapter 4

Finding Core Competency Examples

The will to win, the desire to succeed, the urge to reach your full potential... these are the keys that will unlock the door to personal excellence.

- Confucius

Things to consider

Finding suitable examples to use for the competency questions is often of great concern to candidates. It shouldn't be.

Candidates often doubt themselves and think 'I don't really have an example of dealing with race and diversity, how can I answer this?' or 'I don't really have any good experiences to talk about, other people have volunteered as Police Specials, I haven't done anything like that'.

I'm going to tell you something that may come as a shock. **Your examples are not that important** to the recruiters. To go even further, **your experience isn't that important** to the recruiters. I don't wish to upset people who have put in a great deal of effort and given up personal time to gain these things, because it certainly isn't time wasted, the skills you've gained really do count, within your force, to the people you've helped and to yourself.

As I said earlier, the Police application form is different to any other type of job application. Form technique and **ticking the right boxes is everything to the recruiters** and understanding this is the key to success at this stage. This is one of the main reasons this book was written, to stress to people that they must get their application form technique right and to show them how to do so.

The way the application form is scored has effectively levelled the playing field for candidates. It is possible for someone with no experience to progress to interview stage, while someone who is experienced and ready for the job to be left behind, so follow our method and don't be left behind.

Selecting your examples

You may be asking, so if my examples aren't as important as my form technique, how can I score highly using them and how do I choose them?

Here's how, **choose one example you can use to fit the competency,** even if it only roughly fits. For example, to complete a core competency question you can use anything you've experienced in real life, no matter how insignificant it may seem.

Next, **do not sell yourself short**. Some of the key-phrases that the recruiters are asking for do not always present themselves in this way in real life situations. This doesn't mean you should disadvantage yourself by not mentioning them, you need to bend your experiences around the keywords and vice versa.

It is more than likely that you have actually already met the key-phrase criteria but didn't actually realise because of the way they are worded. For example, you didn't just 'listen to the woman', you 'communicated effectively and empathised, seeing issues from her point of view'.

Below we've included some possible sources of examples to help you choose examples for the different competencies of the form.

Effective Communication
Select a time when you have done one of the following:-

- Communicated instructions.
- Worked in a group.
- Explained something.
- Been in an formal occasion and changed your communication style.

- Put forward an argument.

Examples: Work meetings. Dealing with a difficult customer. A university group assessment. Presenting evidence in court. Training a new staff member. Any type of presentation.

Community and Customer Focus

Select a time when you have done one of the following:-

- Dealt with a customer.
- Worked within the community.
- Had to represent an organisation or company.
- Had to provide a service to someone.

Examples: Resolving an issue for a client or customer. Providing excellent customer service. Dealing with the public on behalf of a company.

Personal Responsibility

Select a time when you have done one of the following:-

- Took on any form of responsibility.
- Made decisions you've had to act on.
- Shown initiative.
- Resolved issues or problems.

Examples: Taking on extra responsibility at work, university or in your personal life. Being placed in any position of authority. Making difficult decisions you have to stand by. Being in charge of any task or undertaking.

Problem Solving
Select a time when you have done one of the following:-

- Dealt with a problem.
- Resolved an issue.
- Had to make a decision based on information you've gathered.
- Solved a complex situation.

Examples: Dealing with an issue at work, university or in your personal life. Completed a task, assignment or responsibility that needed you to gather information. Any tasks or roles that you've taken on that have required you to think before attempting them.

Resilience
Select a time when you have done one of the following:-

- Dealt with a highly stressful situation.
- Dealt with a difficult or emotional challenge.
- Responded to a difficult situation.
- Been in a situation of confrontation.

Examples: Calming or diffusing a situation in your personal, academic or work life. A time when you've been provoked or responded to a confrontational situation, customer or individual. A time when you've remained professional when you could have reacted otherwise.

Respect For Race and Diversity
Select a time when you have done one of the following:-

- Respected the viewpoint of someone from a different, religious, social or cultural background.
- Been sensitive to someone else's needs.

- Challenged inappropriate attitudes.
- Had to deliver a difficult message to someone sensitively.
- Supported someone who is vulnerable.

Examples: Dealing with a conflict between two people with different points of view. Respecting someone else's religious beliefs. Dealing with someone who is different to yourself, whether due to age, opinion, gender, race or appearance. Dealing with with an issue that has involved diversity or material of a sensitive nature.

Teamwork
Select a time when you have done one of the following:-

- Worked as part of a team to complete a task.
- Have built relationships with a group of people and worked towards a common goal.

Examples: A time when you've worked with one or more people on any task within your social, academic or work life.

Keys to success

- Don't be concerned if you can't find the 'perfect' example.

- Remember, the examples themselves are not as important as using the key-phrases when talking about them.

- Adapt your examples and don't sell yourself short - you need to work the key phrases around examples you do have.

- Don't leave key-phrases out, rethink and reshape your answer to include them.

Chapter 5

Answer Structure

Always, always have a plan

— Rick Riordan

We have previously discussed using exact key phrases from your Police Core Competency lists, now we'll provide you with the **exact structure** that will allow you to plan out and answer any Police competency question.

At the moment, all forces are currently using a standardised form, four competency questions, each made up of several questions that address the competency. Each of the four competency questions target an individual competency, at the moment these are 'Effective Communication', 'Resilience', 'Personal Responsibility' and 'Respect for Race and Diversity'.

By following the answer structure in this chapter you will be equipped to deal with Police competency questions even if they differ from our example answers provided.

A useful acronym for structuring answers is S.T.A.R. We will use this structure to answer your competency questions.

Situation & **T**ask	Describe the situation that you found yourself in and what you had to do. You need to **be specific** and chose a single event to talk about as general examples will not suffice. You must describe it in sufficient detail so that the recruiter can understand the situation.
Action	Describe what actions you took. Even if you are part of a group activity, make sure that you are only talking about your own contributions. Be sure to **tell them what you did** and not what you might do.
Result	**Describe the outcome,** how the situation was resolved what happened or what you learned.

Now it's time to apply the concepts we've learned so far to a real core competency question. We'll use the principles of our STAR acronym, an example from the previous chapter and the core competency key words from the application pack.

There are blank spaces within the answer to illustrate how to structure your answers without getting too specific on the example its self. For a full example answer, see the next chapter and beyond.

The core competencies used will be numbered so that you can see exactly where they have been slotted in to the answer. See the core competency section at the back of the book to view the entire list.

PERSONAL RESPONSIBILITY

Q. Please describe a specific situation when you have persevered or have had to put in extra effort in order to complete a task.

A. While working at _____ I had to put in extra effort and persevere in order to take on a role as _____.

Q. How did you approach the situation and make sure that you completed the task?

My approach was to **(3)** take action to resolve problems as they arose in order to fulfil my responsibilities, as well this **(1)** I accepted personal responsibility for the decisions and actions I chose to make. I approached my duties with a sense of **(8)** self motivation and **(5)** pride which ensured that I maintained **(12)** organisational integrity and based my decisions on ethical considerations at time. My positive, **(11)** enthusiastic, honest and genuine attitude meant that I focused on and **(7)** followed tasks through to a satisfactory conclusion whilst **(2)** demonstrating initiative which ensured that I **(4)** did not let colleagues down.

Q. What was particularly good or effective about how you dealt with the situation?

What was particularly effective about my approach was how I ____. By ____ I ensured **(6)** I was conscientious and completed the work on time. I was able to **(9)** focus on tasks even though they were routine and **(10)** furthered my professional knowledge.

Q. What did you consider when dealing with the situation?

I considered ____. **(1)** I was aware of the need to take personal responsibility for my actions and remained professional and calm despite the pressure of the situation, as well as the need to _____.

Q. What difficulties did you experience and how did you overcome them?

What was difficult was ____ which I overcame by **(3)** taking action to resolve problems and ____.

Keys to success

- Be sure to focus on a single example of a time when you've exhibited the key skills.

- Don't give generalisations such as 'I often __' you should always refer directly to your example, 'I did __'.

- Utilise the principles of the S.T.A.R acronym to form the structure of your answers.

- If talking about a group activity be sure to focus on what **YOU** did as a member of the group and not what the team did.

Chapter 6

Example Answer One

Resilience

I have willpower and determination. I am very resilient, like rock.
- Carnie Wilson

So now you have the method to answer any generic competency question provided in the last chapter, it's time for you to see the method in action with some real examples.

You should be able to see just how easy it is to weave together the key-words within the example that you've chosen to use.

You should only use the example answers provided in this book as a base for your own. You should not copy answers from this book but use these examples as foundations for your own.

Q. Please describe a specific example of a time when you have found yourself in a difficult or challenging situation.

What was the situation and why was it difficult or challenging?

Whilst working on a till at a supermarket I was confronted by an angry and aggressive customer who was becoming increasingly agitated and difficult to deal with.

How did you respond and deal with the situation?

I ensured my response maintained my professional ethics whilst under the pressure of the situation, I avoided becoming emotionally involved and instead challenged the hostility and provocation in a calm and restrained way. I thought clearly about the issue, giving the situation my full consideration in order to remain focused and in control. I diffused the customer's anger by engaging him in conversation and addressing his emotional issues in order to move on from the situation, this dealt with his uncertainty and frustration and resolved the issue.

What was particularly good or effective about how you dealt with the situation/people involved?

I effectively dealt with the customer by standing firmly by my position of calming him and managing the tensions and pressures of the situation. By effectively communicating and showing empathy with the man, I was able to remain focused and in control.

What did you consider when dealing with the situation?

I considered how to respond to the anger and aggression and considered the need to respond rationally, without emotion. I also considered the need to give the situation a careful and well thought out approach and resist the pressure to make a quick decision in order to diffuse the situation.

What difficulties did you experience and how did you overcome them?

The man's anger and aggression presented difficulties in dealing with him, I overcame this by responding rationally and standing firm with my calm, restrained approach.

Chapter 7

Example Answer Two

Effective Communication

To effectively communicate, we must realise that we are all different in the way we perceive the world and use this understanding as a guide to our communication with others.
                                                    - Tony Robbins

Q. Please describe a specific situation when you have communicated ideas or information effectively to another person or group of people.

What was the situation and what were the ideas or information you had to communicate?

As part of a final year assessment at university, I carried out a presentation to a large group of peers. I was required to communicate ideas and information effectively and explain research that I had completed.

How did you make sure that you communicated effectively and that your message was understood?

To communicate effectively, I spoke in a confident and authoritative manner, simplifying and explaining difficult concepts to suit my non-technical audience and regularly summarised points so that my message was understood. My presentation slides and notes were concise and well structured to support my arguments and findings. As difficult questions arose, often from group discussions, I was able to listen carefully and deal directly with them using well considered answers and conclusions.

What was particularly good or effective about how you dealt with the situation/people involved.

By effectively tailoring my style of communication to my audience of mixed technical knowledge, I was able to convey information in an appropriate style and clearly explain decisions made and the reasoning behind them in a way that everyone understood and had their questions addressed directly.

What difficulties did you experience and how did you overcome them?
The audience often asked difficult questions regarding my research and findings, however by speaking confidently, listening carefully to questions whilst remaining calm under pressure, I was able to provide direct and well thought out answers.

Chapter 8

Example Answer Three

Personal Responsibility

If I've done something wrong, its up to me to pay the price. It's up to me to make it right.

- Glenn Beck

Q. Please describe a specific situation when you have persevered or have had to put in extra effort in order to complete a task.

Why was it necessary to persevere or put in extra effort?

A senior colleague was taken ill during a marketing campaign which required extra effort to fulfil a senior role as well as my own. This challenge required to persevere and put in extra effort.

How did you approach the situation and make sure that you completed the task?

I accepted personal responsibility for the role and the decisions and actions made within it, this ensured that I saw tasks through to completion and did so in a timely manner. By approaching the role with self motivation, enthusiasm and a sense of pride in the new responsibility I had been given, I ensured that I made decisions based on the organisation's ethical standards and integrity. I adopted a positive attitude and persevered against difficulties encountered which enabled me to complete tasks and not let other colleagues down.

What was particularly good or effective about how you dealt with the situation?

I dealt with the situation effectively by taking a systematic approach to solving problems, often referring to company procedures and behaving in an open, honest and genuine way, which allowed me to complete tasks effectively. I also used my own initiative in dealing with the situation and was able to improve my own professional knowledge and further use this to overcome new challenges as they arose.

What did you consider when dealing with the situation?

I considered the need to keep promises made to senior management in order to not let them down, this involved considering time constraints on completing work, as well as following all tasks through to a satisfactory conclusion. I considered the need to be self motivated as I had been placed in a responsible senior role where I directed the work-flow. It was also apparent that I was personally responsible for my own actions and decisions and that I should approach them with enthusiasm in order to succeed.

What difficulties did you experience and how did you overcome them?

The increased number of responsibilities required me to make a large number of considered decisions which I was able to do by demonstrating enthusiasm, pride, initiative and self motivation.

Chapter 9

Example Answer Four

Respect For Race and Diversity

It is so important to get respect for what you do and at the same time give it.

— Estelle Parsons

Q. Describe a specific situation when you have been required to demonstrate sensitivity or have shown understanding of the needs/views of another person or group of people.

In your response to this question you may draw on your past experience when you have dealt with others who are different from you in any way.

Why was it necessary to demonstrate sensitivity or show understanding?

Whilst working in a car manufacturing plant I had to demonstrate sensitivity and understanding towards two individuals who were arguing over one party's inability to attend an event due to a religious festival. The disagreement arose from differing religious and cultural viewpoints which I had to demonstrate an understanding towards.

How did you deal with the situation and how did you make sure that you demonstrated sensitivity or showed understanding?

By seeing the situation from both viewpoints, I was able to mediate the situation in a polite, tolerant, respectful and dignified way that acknowledged the broad range of cultural beliefs and values that were causing the disagreement. I demonstrated sensitivity towards the issue by challenging the inappropriate attitude and the discriminatory behaviour of one of the individuals in order to support the minority group. By understanding what offended both parties, I was able to adapt my own actions to propose a solution that took in to account the personal needs and interests of both individuals.

What was particularly good or effective about how you dealt with the situation/people involved?

By respecting the needs of everyone involved in the disagreement and showing an understanding towards their problems and vulnerabilities of both parties, I was able to effectively deal with the situation. I was able to use appropriate language that was sensitive to the effect on both parties, considerate to their feelings and helped deliver some difficult messages sensitively.

What did you consider when dealing with the situation?

I considered the need to take in to account the personal needs and interests of both individuals involved in the dispute and to maintain the confidentiality of the situation. I also considered the necessity to give practical support to both parties who may have been feeling vulnerable, as well as approaching the situation in an impartial way that considered both viewpoints.

What difficulties did you experience and how did you overcome them?

I had to challenge difficult and inappropriate attitudes in a sensitive way, I overcame this by being polite, tolerant and patient, treating both individuals with respect and dignity and listening to their viewpoints.

Chapter 10

Further Questions

Police work is a practice in patience.
— Sgt. Harry Howell

What not many people know about this section of the application form is that it isn't actually used for assessment purposes. It's simply another section for the recruiters to assess your handwriting, spelling and grammar.

Despite this I highly recommend that you take the time to put effort in to the questions in this section. A well thought out answer and a continued focus on your writing could tip the recruiter in your favour, it's not certain but it is possible.

We've included some sample answers in order to demonstrate what sort of responses these questions are looking for.

Tell us why you want to become a police officer?

Being a Police Officer has always been an aspiration of mine from a young age and would allow me to help my local community and help people in general. Having personally witnessed the impact good policing can have on people's lives, I want to be able to offer this to others.

Tell us why you have applied to your chosen police force?

This Police force would allow me to make a difference in a local community and be a part of a large and professional organisation who aim to deliver quality service, professional excellence and value for money.

(it is good practice here to use the Police force's slogan, this can usually be found on their website).

Tell us in some detail what tasks do you expect to be undertaking as a police officer?

As a police officer I would expect to undertake tasks that protect the public and community. I would expect to undertake tasks and policing initiatives determined by my force and maintain a visible presence within the community. I expect that I would utilise my skill-set and be personally responsible for the tasks and duties that I carry out both as part of a team of officers and individually.

Tell us what you expect being a police officer to have on your social and domestic life?

The role would impact my domestic and social life due to overtime and unsociable hours, however my excellent time management skills and my realistic expectations of the role would allow me to deal with these challenges.

What preparation have you undertaken before making this application to ensure that you know what to expect and that you are prepared for the role of a Police Officer?

As well as being physically fit and attending the gym, I have volunteered as a Police Special Constable and have experienced what it is like to Police my local community.

Chapter 11

Core Competencies

Nothing endures but personal qualities.
                                    - Walt Whitman

In this section you'll find the Police Core Competencies for 2013.
For application forms later than this date you should check your
forces website in case there have been any changes or
amendments to them as this does happen occasionally.

Community and Customer Focus

Focuses on the customer and provides a high-quality service that is tailored to meet their individual needs. Understands the communities that are served and shows an active commitment to policing that reflects their needs and concerns.

Provides a high level of service to customers. Maintains contact with customers, establishes what they need and responds to them.

Positive Indicators:

1. Accepts personal responsibility for own decisions and actions.

2. Displays initiative, taking on tasks without having to be asked.

3. Takes action to resolve problems and fulfil own responsibilities.

4. Keeps promises and does not let colleagues down.

5. Takes pride in own work.

6. Is conscientious in completing work on time.

7. Follows things through to a satisfactory conclusion.

8. Is self-motivated, showing enthusiasm and dedication to their role.

9. Focuses on a task even if it is routine.

10. Improves own professional knowledge and keeps it up to date.

11. Is open, honest and genuine, standing up for what is right.

12. Makes decisions based upon ethical considerations and organisational integrity.

13. Aware of their own strengths and weaknesses.

Negative Indicators:

1. Is not customer focused and does not consider individual needs.

2. Does not tell customers what is going on.

3. Presents an unprofessional image to customers.

4. Only sees a situation from their own point of view, not from the customers' view.

5. Shows little interest in the customer (e.g. only deals with their immediate problem).

6. Does not respond to the needs of the local community.

7. Slow to respond to customers' requests.

8. Fails to check that customers' needs have been met.

9. Focuses on organisational issues rather than customer needs.

10. Does not make the most of opportunities to talk to people in the community.

Effective Communication

Communicates ideas and information effectively, both verbally and in writing. Uses language and a style of communication that is appropriate to the situation and people being addressed. Makes sure that others understand what is going on.

Communicates all needs, instructions and decisions clearly. Adapts the style of communication to meet the needs of the audience. Checks for understanding.

Positive Indicators:

1. Deals with issues directly.

2. Clearly communicates needs and instructions.

3. Clearly explains management decisions and policy, and the reasons behind them.

4. Communicates face to face wherever possible and if it is appropriate.

5. Speaks with authority and confidence.

6. Changes the style of communication to meet the needs of the audience.

7. Manages group discussions effectively.

8. Summarises information to check that people understand it.

9. Supports arguments and recommendations effectively in writing.

10. Produces well-structured reports and written summaries.

Negative Indicators

1. Is hesitant, nervous and uncertain when speaking.

2. Speaks without first thinking through what to say.

3. Uses inappropriate language or jargon.

4. Speaks in a rambling way.

5. Does not consider the target audience.

6. Avoids answering difficult questions.

7. Does not give full information without being questioned.

8. Writes in an unstructured way.

9. Uses poor spelling, punctuation and grammar.

10. Assumes that others understand what has been said without actually checking.

11. Does not listen, and interrupts at inappropriate times.

Personal Responsibility

Takes personal responsibility for making things happen and achieving results. Displays motivation, commitment, perseverance and conscientiousness. Acts with a high degree of integrity.

Takes personal responsibility for own actions and for resolving issues or problems that arise. Is focused on achieving results to required standards and developing skills and knowledge.

Positive Indicators

1. Accepts personal responsibility for own decisions and actions.

2. Displays initiative, taking on tasks without having to be asked.

3. Takes action to resolve problems and fulfil own responsibilities.

4. Keeps promises and does not let colleagues down.

5. Takes pride in own work.

6. Is conscientious in completing work on time.

7. Follows things through to a satisfactory conclusion.

8. Is self-motivated, showing enthusiasm and dedication to their role.

9. Focuses on a task even if it is routine.

10. Improves own professional knowledge and keeps it up to date.

11. Is open, honest and genuine, standing up for what is right.

12. Makes decisions based upon ethical considerations and organisational integrity.

13. Aware of their own strengths and weaknesses.

Negative Indicators:

1. Passes responsibility upwards inappropriately.

2. Is not concerned about letting others down.

3. Will not deal with issues, and instead just hopes that they will go away.

4. Blames others rather than admitting to mistakes or looking for help.

5. Unwilling to take on responsibility.

6. Puts in the minimum effort that is needed to get by.

7. Shows a negative and disruptive attitude.

8. Shows little energy or enthusiasm for work.

9. Expresses a cynical attitude to the organisation and their job.

10. Gives up easily when faced with problems.

11. Fails to recognise personal weaknesses and development needs.

12. Makes little or no attempt to develop self or keep up to date.

Problem Solving

Gathers information from a range of sources. Analyses information to identify problems and issues and makes effective decisions.

Gathers enough relevant information to understand specific issues and events. Uses information to identify problems and draw logical conclusions. Makes good decisions.

Positive Indicators:

1. Identifies where to get information and gets it.

2. Gets as much information as is appropriate on all aspects of a problem.

3. Separates relevant information from irrelevant information and important information from unimportant information.

4. Takes in information quickly and accurately.

5. Reviews all the information gathered to understand the situation and draw logical conclusions.

6. Identifies and links causes and effects.

7. Identifies what can and cannot be changed.

8. Takes a systematic approach to solving problems.

9. Remains impartial and avoids jumping to conclusions.

10. Refers to procedures and precedents, as necessary, before making decisions.

11. Makes good decisions that take in to account all relevant factors.

Negative Indicators:

1. Does not deal with problems in detail and does not identify underlying issues.

2. Does not gather enough information before coming to conclusions.

3. Does not consult other people who may have extra information.

4. Does not research background.

5. Shows no interest in gathering or using intelligence.

6. Does not gather evidence.

7. Makes assumptions about the facts of a situation.

8. Does not notice problems until they have become significant issues.

9. Gets stuck in the detail of complex situations and cannot see the main issues.

10. Reacts without considering all the angles.

11. Becomes distracted by minor issues.

Resilience

Shows resilience, even in difficult circumstances. Prepared to make difficult decisions and has the confidence to see them through.

Shows reliability and resilience in difficult circumstances. Remains calm and confident, and responds logically and decisively in difficult situations.

Positive Indicators:

1. Is reliable in a crisis, remains calm and thinks clearly.

2. Resolves conflict and deals with hostility and provocation in a calm and restrained way.

3. Responds to challenges rationally, avoiding inappropriate emotion.

4. Deals with difficult emotional issues and then moves on.

5. Manages conflicting pressures and tensions.

6. Maintains professional ethics when confronted with pressure from others.

7. Copes with ambiguity and deals with uncertainty and frustration.

8. Resists pressure to make quick decisions where full consideration is needed.

9. Remains focused and in control of situations.

10. Makes and carries through decisions, even if they are unpopular, difficult or controversial.

11. Stands firmly by a position when it is right to do so.

12. Defends their staff from excessive criticism from outside the team.

Negative Indicators:

1. Gets easily upset, frustrated and annoyed.

2. Panics and becomes agitated when problems arise.

3. Walks away from confrontation when it would be more appropriate to get involved.

4. Needs constant reassurance, support and supervision.

5. Uses inappropriate physical force.

6. Gets too emotionally involved in situations.

7. Reacts inappropriately when faced with rude or abusive people.

8. Deals with situations aggressively.

9. Complains about problems rather than dealing with them.

10. Concedes inappropriately when under pressure.

11. Worries about making mistakes and avoids difficult situations wherever possible.

Respect For Race and Diversity

Considers and shows respect for the opinions, circumstances and feelings of colleagues and members of the public, no matter what their race, religion, position, background, circumstances, status or appearance.

Understands other people's views and takes them into account. Is tactful and diplomatic when dealing with people, treating them with dignity and respect at all times. Understands and is sensitive to social, cultural and racial differences.

Positive Indicators:

1. Sees issues from other people's viewpoints.

2. Is polite, tolerant and patient with people inside and outside the organisation, treating them with respect and dignity.

3. Respects the needs of everyone involved when resolving disagreements.

4. Shows understanding and sensitivity to people's problems and vulnerabilities.

5. Deals with diversity issues and gives positive practical support to staff who may feel vulnerable.

6. Listens to and values others' views and opinions.

7. Uses language in an appropriate way and is sensitive to the way it may affect people.

8. Acknowledges and respects a broad range of social and cultural customs, beliefs and values within the law.

9. Understands what offends others and adapts own actions accordingly.

10. Respects and maintains confidentiality, wherever appropriate.

11. Delivers difficult messages sensitively.

12. Challenges inappropriate attitudes, language or behaviour that is abusive, aggressive or discriminatory.

13. Takes into account others' personal needs and interests. Supports minority groups both inside and outside their organisation.

Negative Indicators:

1. Does not consider other people's feelings.

2. Does not encourage people to talk about personal issues.

3. Criticises people without considering their feelings and motivation.

4. Makes situations worse with inappropriate remarks, language or behaviour.

5. Is thoughtless and tactless when dealing with people.

6. Is dismissive and impatient with people.

7. Does not respect confidentiality.

8. Unnecessarily emphasises power and control in situations where this is not appropriate.

Team-Working

Develops strong working relationships inside and outside the team to achieve common goals. Breaks down barriers between groups and involves others in discussions and decisions.

Works effectively as a team member and helps to build relationships within it. Actively helps and supports others to achieve team goals.

Positive Indicators:

1. Understands own role in a team.

2. Actively supports and assists the team to reach their objectives.

3. Is approachable and friendly to others.

4. Makes time to get to know people.

5. Cooperates with and supports others.

6. Offers to help other people.

7. Asks for and accepts help when needed.

8. Develops mutual trust and confidence in others.

9. Willingly takes on unpopular or routine tasks.

10. Contributes to team objectives no matter what the direct personal benefit may be.

11. Acknowledges that there is often a need to be a member of more than one team.

12. Takes pride in their team and promotes their team's performance to others.

Negative Indicators:

1. Does not volunteer to help other team members.

2. Is only interested in taking part in high-profile and interesting activities.

3. Takes credit for successes without recognising the contribution of others.

4. Works to own agenda rather than contributing to team performance.

5. Allows small exclusive groups of people to develop.

6. Plays one person off against another.

7. Restricts and controls what information is shared.

8. Does not let people say what they think.

9. Does not offer advice or get advice from others.

10. Shows little interest in working jointly with other groups to meet the goals of everyone involved.

11. Does not discourage conflict within the organisation.

Final Words

Please ensure that you check with the Police force that you are applying to, to ensure that you are using the correct Core Competencies as these may vary from force to force.

It is also possible that a small number of forces' questions may differ from those that we have provided answers to in this book. We hope that we have provided you with the necessary tools to adapt your answers to meet these changes.

Finally, we hope all your hard work pays off and that we've helped you on your journey to becoming a Police Officer. You risk your life to make everyone else's safer. Thank you.

www.applicationformpolice.co.uk

Printed in Great Britain
by Amazon.co.uk, Ltd.,
Marston Gate.